INSIDE
MODERN GENETICS

INSIDE
DNA AND RNA

HOWARD PHILLIPS

T0361527

ROSEN
PUBLISHING

NEW YORK

Published in 2021 by The Rosen Publishing Group, Inc.
29 East 21st Street, New York, NY 10010

Copyright © 2022 by The Rosen Publishing Group, Inc.

First Edition

Portions of this work were originally authored by Linley Hall and published as *DNA and RNA*. All new material this edition was authored by Howard Phillips.

Designer: Rachel Rising
Editor: Greg Roza

Cataloging-in-Publication Data

Names: Phillips, Howard, 1971-.
Title: Inside DNA and RNA / Howard Phillips.
Description: New York : Rosen Publishing, 2022. | Series: Inside modern genetics | Includes glossary and index.
Identifiers: ISBN 9781499470376 (pbk.) | ISBN 9781499470383 (library bound) | ISBN 9781499470390 (ebook)
Subjects: LCSH: DNA--Juvenile literature. | RNA--Juvenile literature.
Classification: LCC QP624.P54 2022 | DDC 572.8'6--dc23

Some of the images in this book illustrate individuals who are models. The depictions do not imply actual situations or events.

Manufactured in the United States of America

CPSIA Compliance Information: Batch #CWRYA22. For further information contact Rosen Publishing, New York, New York at 1-800-237-9932.

Find us on

CONTENTS

INTRODUCTION

The human body is made up of tiny units called cells. They're so small that we need a microscope to see them. Scientists aren't sure how many cells make up a typical adult body, but some estimate that it's around 30 trillion!

Cells are not just basic units of life; they're the tiny machinery that keeps us (and all living creatures) alive and growing. Each microscopic cell contains even smaller structures that do important work, such as storing nutrients, making proteins, and creating energy. Perhaps most important to life on Earth, cells contain the genetic material that makes each of us who we are and allows living things to reproduce and thrive: genes, chromosomes, and DNA.

DNA and its helpful friend RNA are very difficult topics to understand. Scientists have made great strides in genetics and the study of DNA over the years, and this book will help you gain a better understanding of what it is and how it works. Let's consider a simple example before we begin.

A student goes to the library in search of a particular piece of information for an essay assignment. They discover that the information they need is contained in a particular chapter of a book. This book is extremely important, and the librarians are afraid of it being damaged, so the library keeps the book in a special room, and no one can take it out of this room. However, the room contains a photocopier. So the student makes a photocopy of the chapter of the book that they need. Then they take the copy into the main part of the library.

The book is also written in Chinese. The student must translate the chapter to English. Using the photocopy, the student sits in the main part of the library and figures out what each of the Chinese characters means. Once the passage is translated, the student can finally write the essay using the information in the chapter.

This analogy describes how deoxyribonucleic acid, or DNA, and ribonucleic acid, or RNA, work together to make proteins. The DNA is the book containing the information. It's kept in a special compartment in the cell called the nucleus, which it can't leave. However, copies of parts of the DNA can be made in the form of RNA. RNA is not an exact copy of the DNA, but it contains the information in the DNA, and RNA (the photocopy) can leave the nucleus.

In the main part of the cell, the RNA is used to create proteins. This process is like translating the chapter from Chinese to English. The components of the RNA molecule are known as nucleotides. They must be translated into amino acids, which are the components of proteins. The proteins carry out the work of the cell. Without functional proteins, a cell can't do its job, and it may die. It's very important that the information contained in the DNA is translated faithfully.

The structure of DNA was discovered in 1953. Before then, there was evidence that it was genetic material, but no one knew how the molecule could carry information. The discovery of the structure made that obvious. Over the last 50 or so years, huge gains have been made in our knowledge about how both DNA and RNA function. These molecules have allowed us to better understand inherited diseases and cancer and create new tests and treatments for them. Discoveries about DNA and RNA have also allowed us to modify organisms through recombinant DNA, by inserting DNA from another organism into the DNA of another organism. In some cases, we have also changed human DNA.

The new technologies that use DNA and RNA have a lot of potential to help people. But they could cause problems as well. We need to be careful as we go into the future. A good understanding of the basics of DNA and RNA is an excellent place to begin. So, let's dive into the microscopic world of genes and DNA

CHAPTER 1

DNA—IT'S IN YOUR GENES

Every living thing contains DNA, from the smallest of micro-organisms to the largest of whales. DNA, or deoxyribonucleic acid, contains the instructions for making proteins. Proteins, in turn, do the work of the cell.

There are two types of cells. Prokaryotic cells are only found in bacteria and archaea. In fact, bacteria and archaea are pro-karyotic cells, since the DNA in prokaryotic cells is mixed in with all the other molecules within the cell.

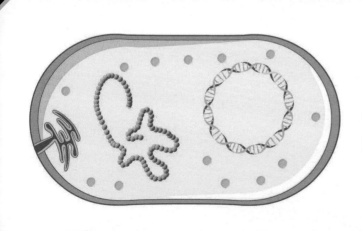

Prokaryotic cells don't have a nucleus. The DNA floats among the other structures in the cell.

Eukaryotic cells are much larger and more complicated than prokaryotic cells. Eukaryotic cells contain a structure called the nucleus where the cell keeps most of its DNA. The nuclear membrane helps protect the DNA from damage. A small amount of DNA is also located in structures called mitochondria and chloroplasts.

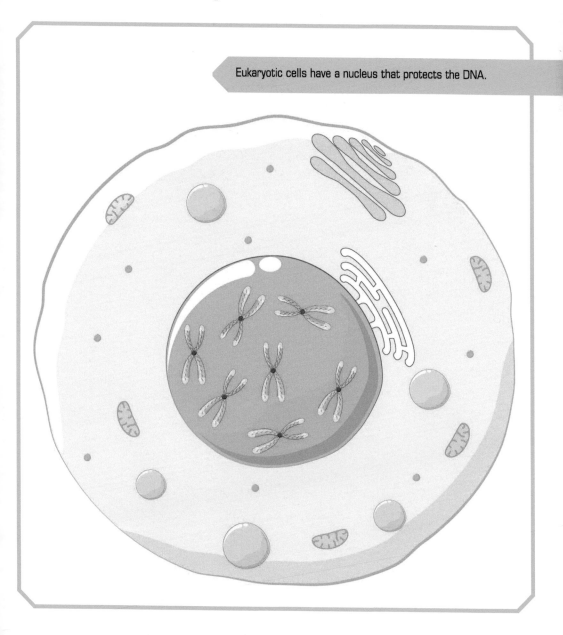

Eukaryotic cells have a nucleus that protects the DNA.

WHAT'S IN DNA?

Nucleic acids are composed of units called nucleotides. Each nucleotide is made from three smaller parts. These are a phosphate group, a sugar, and a nitrogen-containing base. The phosphate group is composed of a phosphorus atom bonded to four oxygen atoms. The sugar in DNA is called deoxyribose. A DNA molecule may contain thousands or even millions of nucleotides. It's composed of a ring of four carbon atoms and one oxygen atom.

The nitrogenous bases are molecules that contain rings of carbon and nitrogen atoms. DNA contains four different bases: adenine, thymine, cytosine, and guanine. These are often abbreviated as A, T, C, and G. Adenine and guanine both have structures that contain two rings. Thymine and cytosine, on the other hand, only contain one ring each.

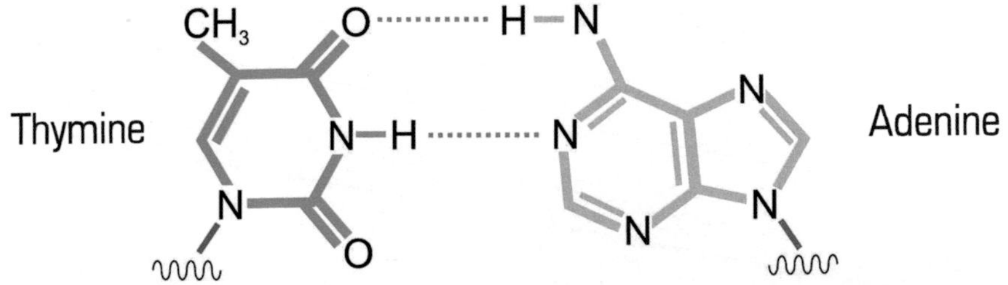

This diagram shows the molecular forms of each of the four nucleotides that make up DNA. These nitrogenous bases join together to form bonds when making DNA.

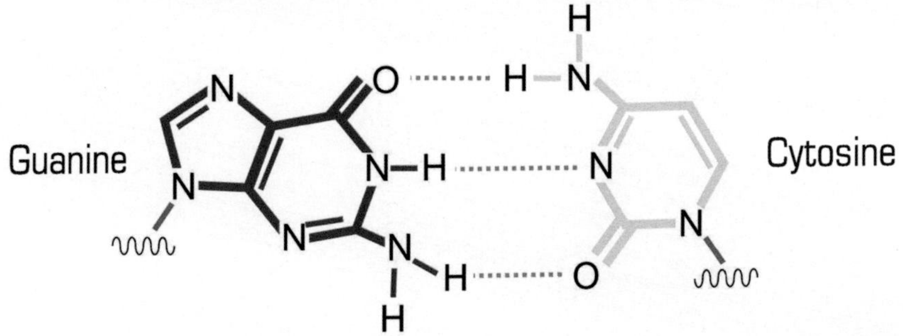

PUTTING DNA TOGETHER

The manner in which these components fit together is important to how DNA functions. A single strand of DNA looks a bit like a comb with the bases as the teeth. Deoxyribose and the phosphate link together in alternation in a long chain to make up the "comb" or backbone of the DNA molecule. The bases are attached to the sugars and seem to hang off the backbone like teeth. The ends of the DNA strand are different. The 3' end (pronounced "three prime end") finishes with a sugar on the backbone, while the 5' end finishes with a phosphate.

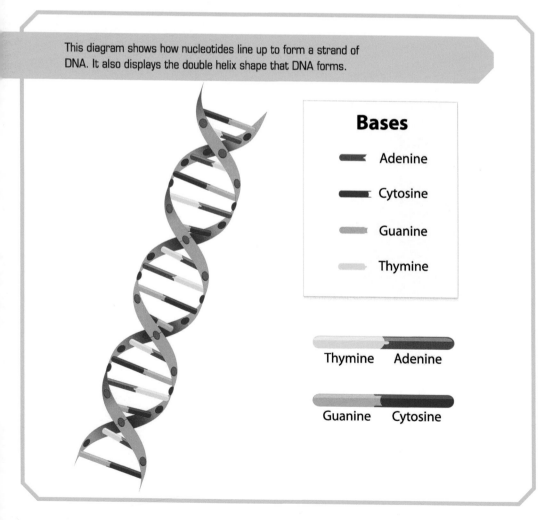

This diagram shows how nucleotides line up to form a strand of DNA. It also displays the double helix shape that DNA forms.

Bases

Adenine

Cytosine

Guanine

Thymine

Thymine   Adenine

Guanine   Cytosine

DNA, however, is not usually single-stranded. Instead, two strands are bound to each other. The backbones run in opposite directions to each other, one being 3' to 5' while the other is 5' to 3'. The bases hanging off the backbone bind to each other to form a shape called a double helix. Adenine on one strand always binds to thymine on the other, and cytosine on one strand always binds to guanine on the other. This means that a base with one ring always binds to a base with two rings. Thus, the A-T and C-G base pairs are about the same size.

An easy way to think about the double helix is as a ladder. The sugar-phosphate backbones are the sides of the ladder. The base pairs are the rungs. This ladder, however, is twisted, so that climbing the rungs of the ladder would feel like going up a spiral staircase.

Perhaps most important, the bases in a DNA molecule aren't in random order. They're in a specific sequence. It's this sequence of A, T, C, and G that contains the instructions for making proteins.

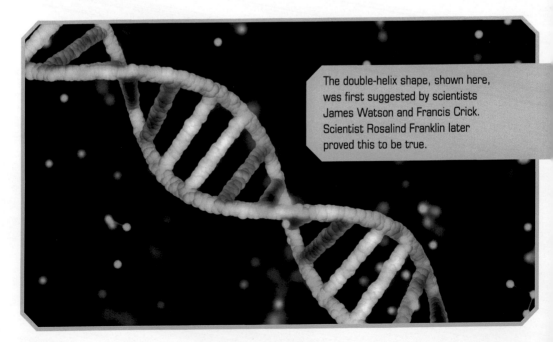

The double-helix shape, shown here, was first suggested by scientists James Watson and Francis Crick. Scientist Rosalind Franklin later proved this to be true.

PACKAGING AND UNPACKING

There are about 3 billion base pairs of DNA in each human cell. Stretched out, this DNA would be more than three feet (0.9 m) long. Cells are obviously much tinier than that, and nuclei are smaller still. To fit in the nucleus, DNA must fold up. This is accomplished with the help of proteins called histones. These proteins allow DNA to become more compact. Wrapping around the histones also helps protect the DNA. When viewed under a microscope, DNA wrapped around histones looks like beads on a string. Around 200 base pairs of DNA wrap around one set of histone proteins.

There are five histone proteins, called H1, H2A, H2B, H3, and H4. H1 binds on its own to about 50 base pairs of DNA. Two copies of each of the other four histone proteins combine to create what's called the histone octamer. About 150 base pairs of DNA wrap twice around this octamer.

In cells, DNA wrapped around histones rarely looks like beads on a string. Instead, the histones pack together to condense the DNA even further. This helps store the DNA, but it must be "unpacked," or unwound, for replication and other genetic processes.

WHAT ARE CHROMOSOMES?

The DNA in eukaryotic cells isn't connected in one long strand. It's divided into smaller strands called chromosomes. Each type of organism has its own unique number of chromosomes. Humans have 46. The butterfly species *Polyommatus atlanticus* (also called Atlas blue) has around 225 chromosomes! Many other butterfly species only have 10 chromosomes. However, the number of chromosomes has nothing to do with the complexity of an organism or how much DNA it has.

Chromosomes have two forms: linear and circular. Humans and other complex organisms have linear chromosomes. Many bacteria have circular chromosomes. Bacteria are prokaryotes, so their DNA isn't contained in a nucleus. Storing the DNA in a circular form helps keep it safe.

Most humans have 46 chromosomes in 23 pairs. In each pair, one chromosome comes from the mother and one from the father. One pair of chromosomes varies according to sex. Females have two X chromosomes, while males have one X and one Y chromosome. The 22 nonsex chromosomes are

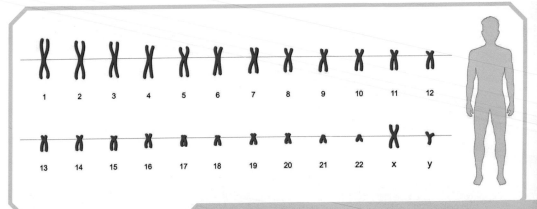

The X and Y chromosomes are often called the "sex chromosomes." They usually determine biological sex, reproductive organs, and sexual characteristics that develop in a person.

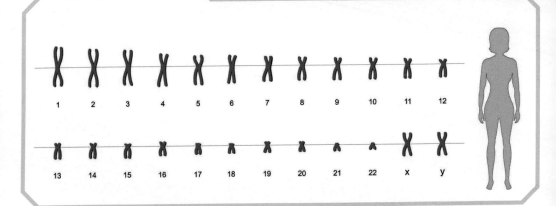

numbered roughly according to their length. Chromosome 1 is the longest, while chromosome 21 is the smallest (22 is slightly longer than 21).

DISCOVERING THE STRUCTURE OF DNA

In the early 1950s, many scientists were exploring the structures of molecules essential to living things. They had determined that DNA was the material of heredity. Without knowing its structure, however, scientists couldn't figure out how DNA carried information.

In early 1953, Linus Pauling published a paper on DNA's structure. He suggested that it was composed of three strands with their backbones bound together in the middle and their bases on the outside. James Watson and Francis Crick, who had also been working on the problem, knew that Pauling's model had to be wrong. They proposed the double-helix structure that we now know to be correct. Watson and Crick determined the structure based on many pieces of information. One was x-ray patterns taken of DNA crystals by Rosalind Franklin. Known as Photo 51, the pattern showed that DNA had to be a helix. Watson and Crick also knew that experiments in Erwin Chargaff's laboratory showed that the bases adenine and thymine occurred in equal amounts, as did cytosine and guanine. This suggested that these bases were paired somehow.

The two scientists built models of DNA. These visual aids helped Watson and Crick figure out how the helix was put together. Other scientists involved with the issue quickly accepted their findings as accurate. The two, along with Maurice Wilkins, received the Nobel Prize for their work in 1962. Sadly, by that time Franklin had died of cancer.

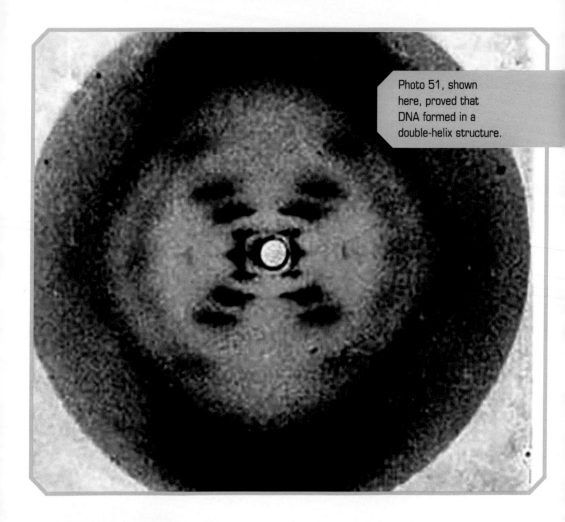

Photo 51, shown here, proved that DNA formed in a double-helix structure.

DNA AT WORK

The parts of DNA known as genes are units of heredity and contain the instructions to make proteins. Most eukaryotic organisms carry two copies of each gene, one on each pair of chromosomes. One gene is inherited from the mother and one from the father. Different forms of the same gene, called alleles, can make an organism have different characteristics.

Between 1856 and 1863, a monk named Gregor Mendel used pea plants to work out the basic rules of heredity. In his experiments, he found that some pea seeds were smooth while

Gregor Mendel was a Czech scientist and Augustinian monk. Starting around 1854, Mendel carried out his genetics experiments on pea plants at St. Thomas's Abbey in Brno, Czech Republic (then Moravia).

others were wrinkled, some yellow while others were green, and so on. He thought that each plant contained factors inherited from the parent plants that determined these characteristics. Later, when scientists studied DNA, they realized that the factors that Mendel described were actually genes in the DNA sequence.

Only 1 percent of human DNA is made up of genes. The other 99 percent is "noncoding" DNA. Noncoding DNA is sometimes called "junk" DNA. This type of DNA doesn't contain the "code," or instructions, for creating proteins. Some noncoding DNA helps signal where the genes are located and when they should be translated into proteins. The functions of other sections of DNA are largely unknown. Researchers first thought that the DNA outside of genes was worthless. Now they are realizing just how important some of this DNA is.

Every cell in an organism should contain exactly the same DNA. Making exact copies isn't easy, but cells use many tools to make sure that it happens—most of the time. The next chapter looks at replication, the process in which strands of DNA are copied.

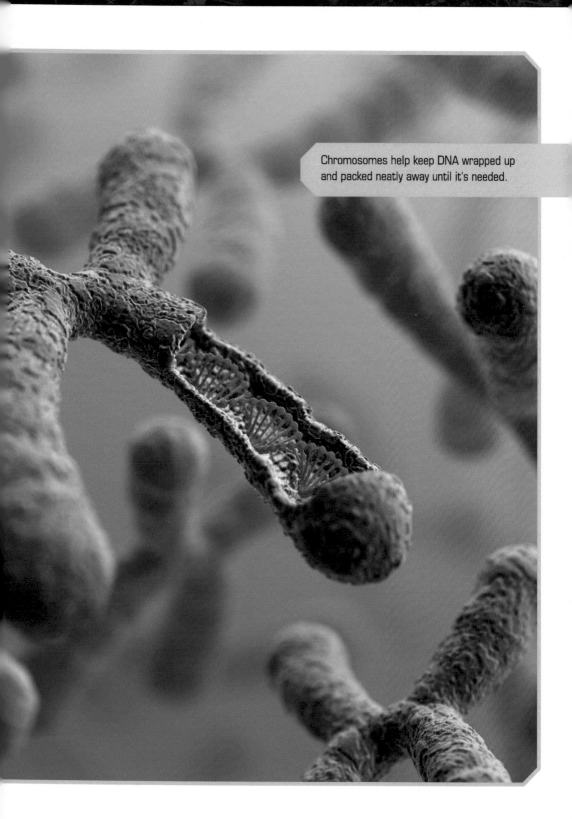

Chromosomes help keep DNA wrapped up and packed neatly away until it's needed.

CHAPTER 2

DNA REPLICATION

Among the many other things they do, cells also divide to create new cells. This cell division is important for growth, which allows living things to increase in size and become older. Cells also eventually get old and die. Cell division helps make sure that young cells are available to take the place of the old ones. People scrub off old, dead skin cells during everyday activities. But they don't run out of skin because new skin cells are created constantly.

A cell makes a copy of its DNA when it divides. This process is called replication. DNA replication is described as semiconservative. Each new DNA double helix contains one old DNA strand and one new one. The old one serves as a template for creating the new strand.

MITOSIS AND MEIOSIS

The nuclear division that happens in most cells of the body is called mitosis. This process creates two new nuclei that are identical to the original nucleus. This means the cell replicates all the DNA in its nucleus. Each new cell has its own complete set of genetic code. After replication of the DNA, the nuclear membrane disintegrates. The two sets of chromosomes are pulled to opposite ends of the cell. New nuclear membranes then form, and the cell divides, creating two new cells.

Some cells in the body divide by meiosis. This process only happens in the sex organs, and it creates sex cells. The sex cells are called eggs, or ova, in those who are biologically female, and sperm in those who are biologically male. To create a new organism, one sperm combines with one egg. This combined cell, called the zygote, needs to have the usual number of chromosomes for that particular species—46 in humans.

During mitosis, a cell's DNA is replicated and organized in the middle of the cell. The two copies are pulled in different directions as the cell divides to create two new cells.

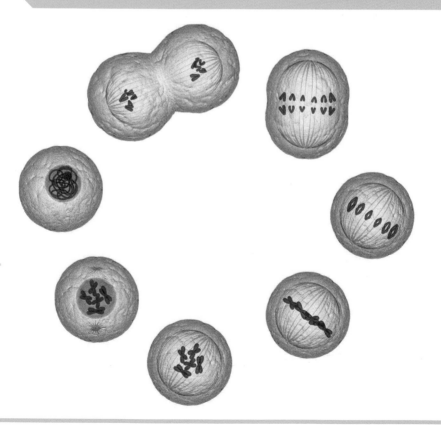

Thus, each sex cell needs to have half that number—usually 23 in humans.

Meiosis is similar to mitosis at the start. All the DNA in the nucleus is replicated. Then, however, the pairs of chromosomes line up so they look like two letter Xs beside each other because each old chromosome and its new copy are still connected at the middle. Now the chromosomes have an opportunity to swap DNA. For example, a portion of each chromosome 19 might break off and reattach to the other chromosome 19. This helps increase genetic diversity. At this point, the pairs of chromosomes separate into two nuclei, cutting the number of chromosomes in each daughter nucleus in half. Each of these two new nuclei goes through another round of division. Meiosis and division of the cells yield four sex cells that contain half the usual number of chromosomes.

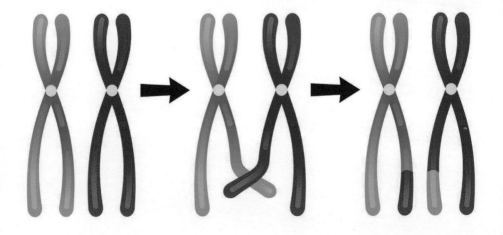

During meiosis, pairs of chromosomes may swap sections of DNA, as shown here. This results in greater genetic diversity.

REPLICATING DNA

Enzymes enter the nucleus during cell division to signal to the DNA that it's time to replicate. Enzymes are protein catalysts that speed up reactions. They bring together molecules and help them interact. These particular enzymes help the DNA unwind from the histones. This makes the DNA more **accessible** for replication.

Next, proteins called initiators scan the DNA strands. They search for sequences called origins, which are the places where DNA replication must start. An organism's DNA may contain up to 100,000 origins. This means replication occurs at many places at the same time, speeding up the process.

Once an initiator locates an origin, it breaks apart the two DNA strands, separating the complementary bases. Then an enzyme called helicase opens the DNA even farther. It may separate hundreds of base pairs. Single-stranded binding proteins attach to the DNA to help it stay open. Another protein called gyrase helps prevent the DNA from becoming twisted. At each end of the bubble of open DNA there's a replication fork where the DNA goes from being single-stranded to double-stranded. Let's focus on what happens at just one of these forks. One strand runs toward the fork in the 5' to 3' direction. It's known as the leading strand. The other strand is known as the lagging strand.

One or more nucleotides of temporary RNA, known as primers, bond to the bases first opened in the origin. Primers help get things moving. A protein called DNA polymerase then begins to move down the leading strand. As it goes, it determines the next base in line and attaches the complementary nucleotide. Lots of these nucleotides are floating in the nucleus, ready to become part of the DNA strand.

Unfortunately, DNA polymerase only works in the 5' to 3' direction. As more bases open up at the replication fork, the DNA of the lagging strand is replicated in the 5' to 3' direction in short bursts known as Okazaki fragments. Each fragment gets its own RNA primers.

Eventually, the DNA polymerase on the leading strand reaches the next origin, where replication has already occurred. Enzymes then remove the RNA primers and the appropriate DNA nucleotides are inserted. The protein ligase then links all the new DNA strands. This process of replication within a single human cell can take several hours.

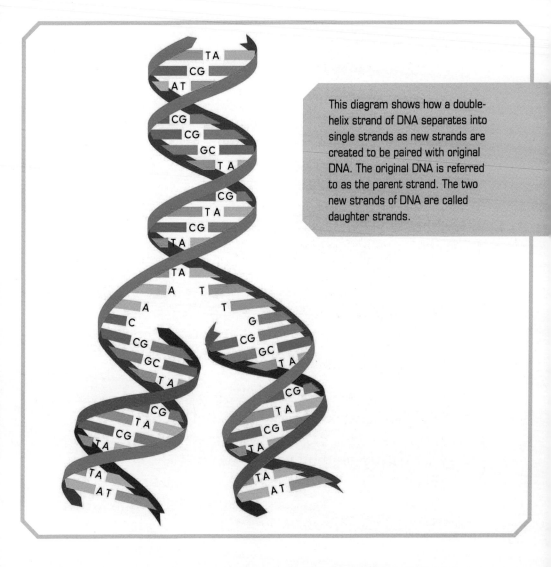

This diagram shows how a double-helix strand of DNA separates into single strands as new strands are created to be paired with original DNA. The original DNA is referred to as the parent strand. The two new strands of DNA are called daughter strands.

THE HUMAN GENOME PROJECT

A genome is an organism's entire complement of DNA. In humans, this encompasses chromosomes 1 through 22, plus the X and Y chromosomes. The Human Genome Project was an international collaboration between scientists working to find the sequence of bases in human DNA. The project began in 1990. The rough draft of the human genome was released in the year 2001 and the final draft in 2003. Since then, researchers have used the information in many experiments.

DNA replication was a key focus of the Human Genome Project. It allowed researchers to determine the sequence of the DNA. The sequencing method is known as the chain termination or Sanger method, named after its inventor, Frederick Sanger

Dideoxynucleotides are similar to regular DNA nucleotides, except they lack one of the chemical groups that help the normal deoxynucleotides link to one another. Once a dideoxynucleotide is incorporated into a DNA strand, replication stops because there's nothing for the next nucleotide to attach to. Dideoxynucleotides can be labeled with fluorescent dyes that make them glow different colors, making them easier to identify.

To sequence a DNA sample of interest, scientists combine lots of copies of the DNA of interest, the RNA and proteins necessary for replication, regular DNA nucleotides, and small amounts of the fluorescent dideoxynucleotides. As replication progresses, usually regular nucleotides will be incorporated. But sometimes a dideoxynucleotide will be added to the growing strand. Replication will stop at this point. This creates DNA strands of many different lengths.

(continued on next page)

(continued from previous page)

After replication finishes, scientists use a technique called gel electrophoresis to separate the strands according to their size. An electrical current is used to move DNA fragments through a gel. Smaller fragments move faster than larger fragments. Strands of the same size line up as a band at a different place in the gel. Each band glows a different color depending on the dideoxynucleotide it contains. Using these colors, researchers can read the DNA sequence along the gel.

Improvements in technology continue to make genome sequencing faster and cheaper. In 2007, scientists in Houston, Texas, gave James Watson, codiscoverer of the DNA structure, a DVD that contained his own genome sequence! This was a breakthrough in making the process less expensive—it was the first individual genome to be sequenced for under $1 million. Eventually, genome sequencing will likely be inexpensive enough for everyone to do it.

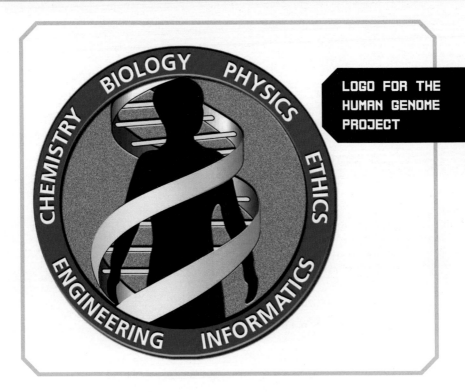

LOGO FOR THE HUMAN GENOME PROJECT

LOOSE ENDS

DNA replication is generally fast and accurate. However, mistakes happen. Occasionally, DNA polymerase mismatches bases—for example, it might pair a thymine with a guanine. An enzyme called proofreading DNA polymerase looks for mismatched bases in the new DNA strand. When it finds errors, it removes the wrong nucleotide and inserts the correct one. The cell also needs to clean up the ends of the chromosomes. The ends of chromosomes are known as telomeres. The DNA in telomeres does not code for proteins. Instead, telomeres protect the important information in the DNA molecule. After replication, the DNA has single-stranded ends. In meiosis, an enzyme called telomerase adds more bases to the end of the DNA so that it is entirely double-stranded. In contrast, in mitosis these single-stranded ends are just chopped off. Thus, the telomeres get shorter every time the cell divides. When the telomeres get too short, the cell dies. This is part of normal aging.

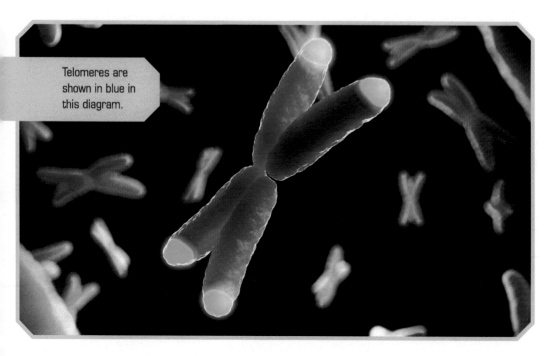

Telomeres are shown in blue in this diagram.

CHAPTER 3

WHAT IS RNA?

Although DNA is crucial to health and development, it can't direct the activities of the cell without the help of RNA. RNA is an abbreviation for ribonucleic acid. It's similar to DNA in many ways. RNA and DNA contain many of the same components, but RNA is a more versatile molecule than DNA. It can do things that DNA can't.

RNA is made in the nucleus of the cell. DNA is used as the template for manufacturing RNA. The process is known as transcription, and chapter 4 will explain it in more depth. After being made in the nucleus, RNA moves into the cytoplasm to do its work.

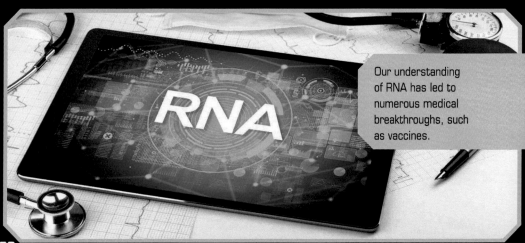

Our understanding of RNA has led to numerous medical breakthroughs, such as vaccines.

INSIDE RNA

As with DNA, RNA nucleotides contain a phosphate, a sugar, and a base. The phosphate is exactly the same. The sugar in RNA, however, is ribose. It contains one more oxygen atom than deoxyribose, the sugar in DNA. (Indeed, the "deoxy" in deoxyribose indicates that it's ribose that's missing an oxygen atom.)

This illustration shows the structure of RNA. Note how it's a single strand and not the double-helix shape of DNA.

RNA also contains four nitrogenous bases. Three of these are the same as in DNA: guanine, cytosine, and adenine. However, RNA contains the base uracil instead of thymine. The structures of uracil and thymine are similar, and uracil prefers to bond with adenine. However, uracil can bond to cytosine and guanine as well. This is an important characteristic.

WHAT'S THE DIFFERENCE?

RNA has two traits that make it more reactive than DNA: ribose instead of deoxyribose, and uracil instead of thymine. Why is it important for RNA to be more reactive than DNA? DNA's function is to keep the genetic material safe. Being less likely to react with other molecules is important. On the other hand, RNA needs to react with other molecules as it fulfills its function of making proteins.

Another significant difference between RNA and DNA has to do with their structures. DNA is a double-stranded molecule. RNA is almost always a single-stranded molecule. This makes it less stable than DNA. After RNA has fulfilled its function, it falls apart. The nucleotides are then used to make other RNA molecules.

RNA's single strand can fold into far more shapes than DNA can. This is where the ability of uracil to bond with any of the other bases comes in handy. Uracil's bonding helps RNA remain in different shapes. These shapes depend on what the particular RNA molecule's function is. In addition, some RNA molecules contain sequences that are complementary. The RNA can thus fold over and form a double-stranded molecule with itself. This helps increase the stability of the RNA when that's important for its function.

DNA is made up of two strands, which form a double-helix shape. RNA usually has just one strand.

RNA

DNA

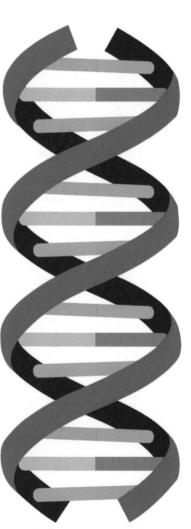

TYPES OF RNA

All types of RNA are created using DNA as a template. This is known as transcription. However, after transcription the various RNAs fold into different shapes and fulfill very distinct functions. There are many different types of RNA. The three most common types are known as messenger RNA (mRNA), transfer RNA (tRNA), and ribosomal RNA (rRNA).

This three-dimensional rendering shows several kinds of RNA (orange, yellow) as they unwind a strand of DNA (purple) to create a strand of RNA (red).

WHICH CAME FIRST?

Many scientists used to wonder: Why not just make proteins directly from DNA? Why do we even need RNA? Several decades ago, Francis Crick, one of the discoverers of the structure of DNA, suggested that RNA existed before DNA. When life was just beginning on Earth, he theorized, organisms used RNA to encode their genetic material instead of DNA. Crick thought that this early RNA was able to catalyze its own replication. In Crick's theory, DNA was a later development in the evolution of life. Its more stable structure helped organisms protect their genetic material better than RNA could.

In the early 1980s, scientists Thomas Cech and Sidney Altman showed that some RNA can catalyze reactions. Then, in the 1990s, Harry Noller showed that the RNA in the ribosome actually links amino acids together into a protein. Previously, scientists had thought that the proteins in the ribosome did this. These discoveries help support the idea that RNA existed before DNA even evolved. Today, most scientists believe that RNA came before DNA, though we may never know for sure.

Messenger RNA is a transcript of a gene. This means that each mRNA molecule carries the instructions for making a protein. After it's made in the nucleus through the process of transcription, mRNA travels into the cytoplasm to a ribosome.

Ribosomes are the parts of a cell where proteins are made. They are composed of about 65 percent ribosomal RNA and 35 percent protein. Some ribosomes are attached to another structure in the cell called the endoplasmic reticulum. Others float around in the cytoplasm. Ribosomes have two subunits, a small one and a large one. The mRNA slides through the small subunit, which reads it. The large subunit builds the corresponding protein.

Transfer RNA carries amino acids to the ribosome. Amino acids are the building blocks of proteins. On one end of the tRNA molecule is a site where an amino acid can attach. A family of enzymes called aminoacyl tRNA synthetases attaches the amino acids to the appropriate tRNA molecules.

There is a sequence of three bases on the other end of the tRNA known as an anticodon, which is complementary to a sequence of three bases in the messenger RNA. This mRNA sequence is known as a codon. The amino acid attachment site is specific to the amino acid that corresponds to the codon that matches the tRNA's anticodon. The codon for the amino acid methionine, for example, is AUG. The anticodon on the tRNA that carries methionine is UAC. The ribosome matches the codons and anticodons when it puts together a new protein. The next chapter will explain this process, which is called translation.

RNA molecules can also help regulate genes. In eukaryotes, small RNAs known as microRNAs can prevent messenger RNA from being translated or make mRNA degrade faster. This process is called RNA interference. In prokaryotes, RNA bases known as CRISPR RNAs perform a similar function. Some cells contain antisense RNA, which is complementary to strands of mRNA. The antisense RNA binds to the mRNA, which prevents it from being translated. This is one way that cells control how much of certain proteins is made. In addition, small nuclear RNA is found in spliceosomes. These complexes of protein and snRNA help process other types of RNA after they are transcribed. Scientists are still learning about all the different types of RNA and the functions they can perform.

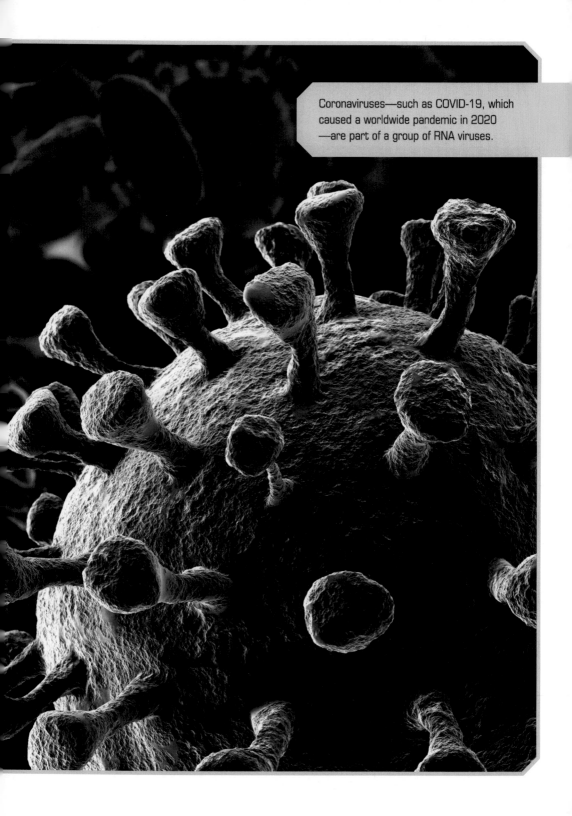

Coronaviruses—such as COVID-19, which caused a worldwide pandemic in 2020 —are part of a group of RNA viruses.

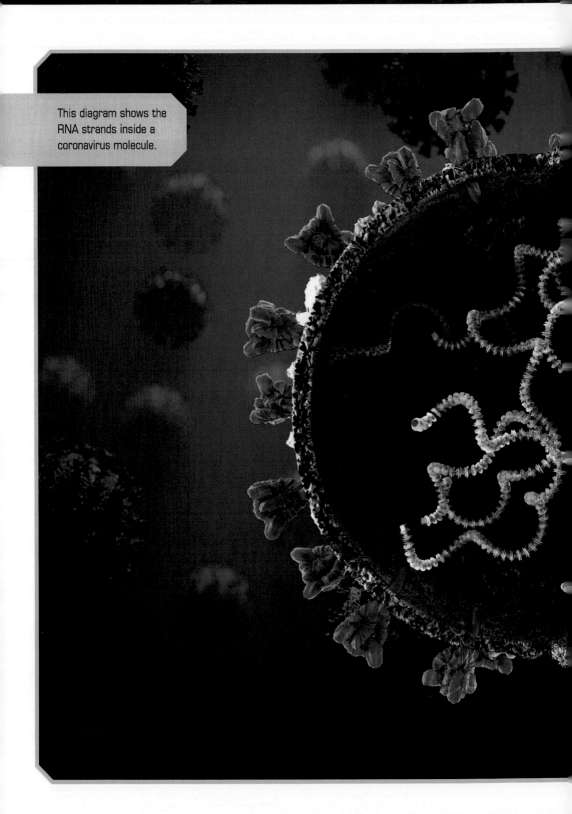

This diagram shows the RNA strands inside a coronavirus molecule.

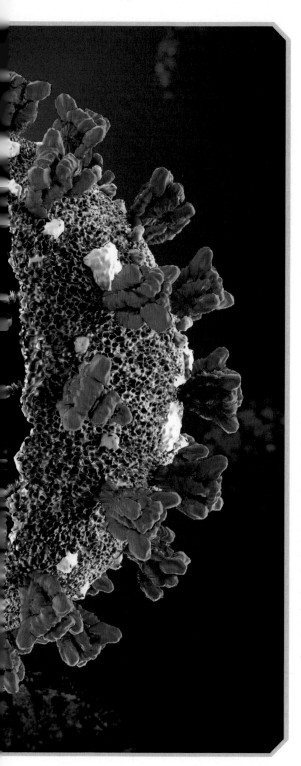

RNA VIRUSES

Some viruses use RNA instead of DNA as their genetic material. Viruses are not cells. Rather, they're basically a shell made out of protein around some nucleic acid, either DNA or RNA. Viruses are parasites. They hijack cells in order to reproduce themselves. Many viruses cause disease. The human immunodeficiency virus (HIV), which causes AIDS, is an RNA virus.

In organisms, DNA serves as the template to make RNA. But RNA-based viruses contain a protein called reverse transcriptase. Once a virus enters a cell, this enzyme can make single-stranded DNA using RNA as a template. Then the virus makes double-stranded DNA from the single strand. Finally, the virus inserts its DNA into the host cell's genome. The cell then starts making viral proteins from this DNA.

CHAPTER 4

A CLOSER LOOK AT TRANSCRIPTION AND TRANSLATION

Transcription is the process in which RNA molecules are made from DNA. Translation is the process in which this RNA is used to create proteins. Both of these processes are essential to the life of the cell—as well as life on Earth.

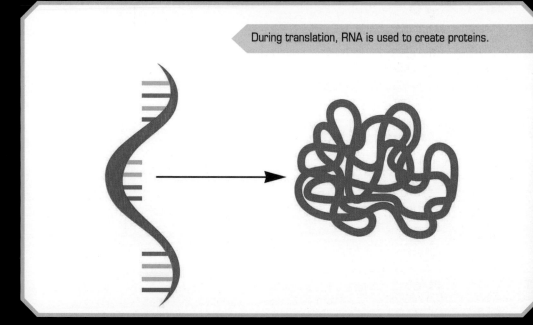

During translation, RNA is used to create proteins.

THE PROCESS OF TRANSCRIPTION

During transcription, DNA serves as a template to make RNA. However, since RNA contains some different components from DNA, transcription doesn't create an exact copy the way replication does. But the RNA created in transcription contains the information in the DNA sequence. The base sequence in the RNA corresponds to the base sequence in the DNA. This is the most important part.

Molecules of mRNA, tRNA, and rRNA are all formed by the same transcription process. At the beginning of transcription, a group of proteins called a holoenzyme complex scans the DNA, looking for the promoter sequence of the gene to be transcribed. The promoter is often a TATA box, so called because it contains a repeating T-A-T-A sequence.

During transcription, RNA molecules are made from DNA.

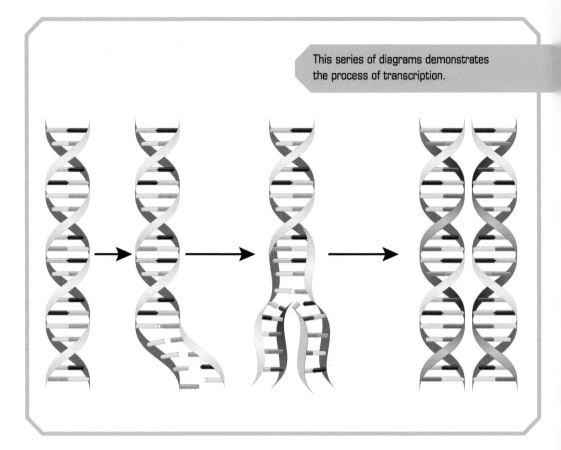

This series of diagrams demonstrates the process of transcription.

    The holoenzyme complex binds to the promoter and makes a small break in the DNA. This allows the enzyme RNA polymerase to access the base pairs. RNA polymerase breaks apart about 20 base pairs, creating a bubble in the DNA. Then it uses RNA nucleotides floating in the nucleus to create a strand of RNA that's complementary to the DNA. This process, called elongation, causes the RNA strand to grow longer.

    As the RNA strand grows, it's pushed away from the DNA, and the bubble closes. Only a bubble of about 20 base pairs is open at one time. This helps protect the DNA. Eventually, the RNA polymerase reaches a terminator sequence in the DNA. This sequence signals that the end of the gene has been reached. The RNA detaches from the DNA, and the DNA closes fully.

POST-TRANSCRIPTION

At this point, the RNA strand is not yet ready. Almost every eukaryotic gene contains sequences called exons and introns. The exons are the parts that code for protein and are most important. They were named "exons" because they are the parts of the genetic material that "express," or convey, the code needed for replication. The introns are intervening sequences that don't code for protein. Introns come in between exons and "interfere" with their work. Therefore, introns must be removed. Researchers are not sure what the purpose of introns is. Some have dismissed them as junk DNA that is completely useless. Others think that at least some introns may be important in regulating processes involving DNA. More research is needed to understand these sequences.

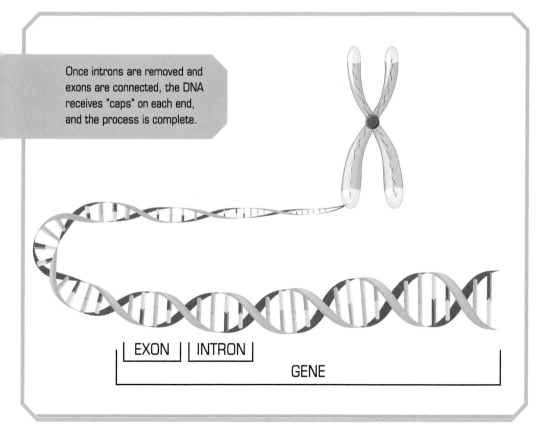

Once introns are removed and exons are connected, the DNA receives "caps" on each end, and the process is complete.

EXON INTRON

GENE

A complex of RNA and protein subunits called a spliceo-some removes the introns and binds the ends of the exons together. Researchers used to think that one gene always yields one protein. However, we now know that isn't true. The spliceosome can edit the RNA in different ways. By leaving out one or more exons, it can create different proteins. Human genes are particularly good at this. This efficient editing is one reason why human beings don't have as many genes as one would expect for such a complex organism. Many human genes can produce multiple proteins, so fewer genes are needed.

After intron removal, the RNA also receives a guanine cap on its leading end and an adenine cap on its tail. These help prevent the RNA from falling apart too quickly. The RNA is now ready to leave the nucleus and get to work.

THE PROCESS OF TRANSLATION

During translation, the information in the mRNA is used to create a protein. Most organisms, including humans, use a set of 20 different amino acids to make proteins. Scientists found that a sequence of three bases on an mRNA molecule corresponds to one amino acid. These triplets of bases are called codons.

There are 64 different codons. Some amino acids are coded for by more than one codon, but no codons respond to more than one amino acid. One codon, AUG, is the start signal, but it also codes for the amino acid methionine. Therefore, all proteins start with methionine at first, though it's sometimes removed later. In addition, three codons don't code for any amino acids at all. These codons—UAG, UAA, and UGA—are the stop signals.

At the beginning of the process of translation, mRNA forms a complex with the small subunit of a ribosome. The mRNA slides along the subunit until the start codon, AUG, reaches the active site. Next, a tRNA molecule carrying a methionine joins the complex.

After the tRNA carrying methionine binds its anticodon to the mRNA start codon, the large subunit of the ribosome links up to the small subunit. The large subunit of the ribosome contains three slots called A, P, and E. tRNA molecules fit in the A and P slots such that their anticodons line up with the codons of the mRNA. When the subunits link up, the methionine tRNA starts out in the P slot of the large subunit.

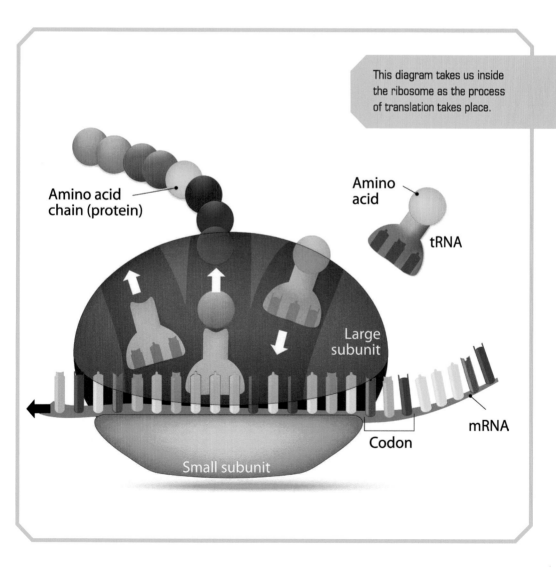

This diagram takes us inside the ribosome as the process of translation takes place.

Amino acid chain (protein)

Amino acid

tRNA

Large subunit

mRNA

Codon

Small subunit

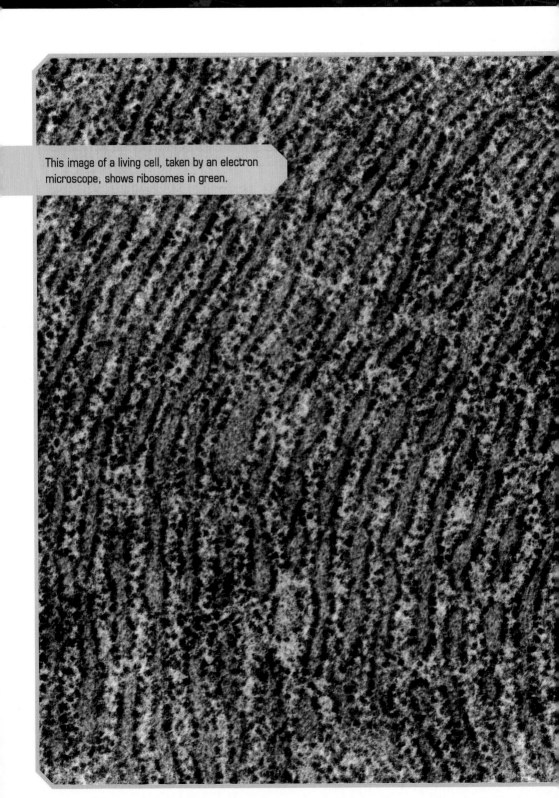

This image of a living cell, taken by an electron microscope, shows ribosomes in green.

Let's say that the second codon on the mRNA is GGG, which codes for glycine. A glycine-carrying tRNA with the anticodon CCC would enter the A slot of the ribosome. Ribosomal RNA then bonds the two amino acids together. In this process, the methionine is detached from its tRNA in the first slot. That tRNA moves to the E slot and then leaves the ribosome to pick up another methionine from the cytoplasm. The mRNA slides over, and the glycine tRNA slides with it, moving from the A slot to the P slot. Then, another tRNA can slide into the A slot. This process repeats over and over to elongate the amino acid chain. This chain hangs off one of the tRNA molecules in the ribosome. It's passed from tRNA to tRNA as the chain gets longer.

Eventually, the ribosome reaches a stop codon. No tRNAs have anticodons that correspond to stop codons. Proteins called release factors recognize the stop signal and detach the protein product from the final tRNA. Other proteins help the new amino acid chain fold into a functional protein. Then the protein goes off to do its work. The last tRNA exits the ribosome so that all slots are empty.

The ribosome is then ready to create a new protein. The tRNA molecules are also reused over and over. The mRNA may be read multiple times depending on how much of a particular protein is needed. It usually disintegrates relatively quickly, however.

Transcription and translation are both essential processes in a cell. But how does a cell know which genes to translate, and when to do it? What happens if a mistake is made during the process? The next chapter looks at how cells control the expression of genes.

THE CODON CODE

Researchers knew that DNA makes RNA, which makes protein, by the late 1950s. They had also discovered the structure of DNA. However, it wasn't clear how nucleic acids were translated into amino acids. With only four bases in RNA (C, G, A, and U) and 20 amino acids, each base couldn't code for one amino acid. Pairs of amino acids could not be right either because there were only 16 possibilities. But triplets of amino acids gives a total of 64 possibilities, many more than necessary.

Francis Crick and Sydney Brenner established that the code is made of triplets. They found that if they deleted one, two, or four base pairs from a gene, they ended up with nonfunctional proteins. If they deleted three bases, however, one amino acid would be missing, but the rest of the protein would be normal.

Then, Marshall Nirenberg and Heinrich Matthaei created an mRNA strand made of uracil. This yielded a protein that was made entirely of the amino acid phenylalanine. Therefore, the triplet UUU had to translate to phenylalanine. A variety of other experiments were conducted to determine the other triplets.

As researchers had expected, many triplets coded for the same amino acid. Often, these codons differ just in their last letter. For example, the codons GCT, GCA, GCG, and GCC all code for the amino acid alanine. Researchers now think that the first and second letters in a triplet are examined most closely during protein synthesis. In additions, investigations showed that only 61 codons correspond to amino acids. The other three signal for translation to stop. It took several years, but scientists eventually cracked the code.

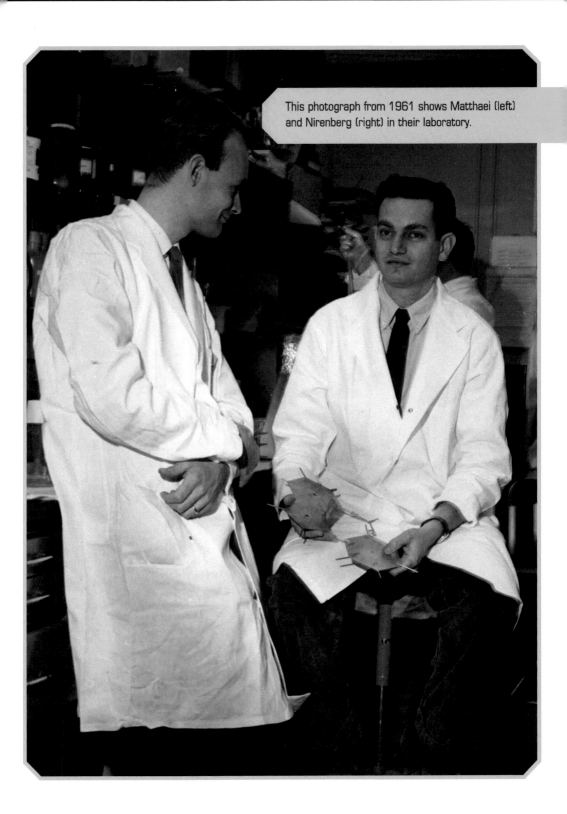

This photograph from 1961 shows Matthaei (left) and Nirenberg (right) in their laboratory.

CHAPTER 5

GENE REGULATION AND MUTATION

Humans cells come in more than 200 different types. Sex cells contain only half of an organism's number of chromosomes. Red blood cells don't have nuclei or DNA, but all other human cell types contain a complete set of DNA, which is usuaully 46 chromosomes. Therefore, all cells (except for red blood cells) contain the instructions for making every protein an organism could want to make.

However, most cells don't need to make all those proteins. A muscle cell and a skin cell obviously have different functions, and they need different proteins to carry out these functions. As a result, different genes are active in skin cells and muscle cells. Genes that are unnecessary in a particular type of cell are turned off early in development. Even within a certain type of cell, however, different genes may be more or less active at different times.

Gene regulation is the process by which cells turn genes off and on at different times. Regulation is a response to a variety of factors. The processes that prokaryotes and eukaryotes use to regulate genes are different, but basic idea is the same: A protein should only be made when it's needed.

PROKARYOTIC CELL REGULATION

Prokaryotes such as bacteria are single-celled organisms. This means that shutting off genes due to cell specialization isn't an issue. However, prokaryotes turn genes off and on depending on their environment. For example, when a particular nutrient is available, bacteria may activate genes that code for proteins that digest that nutrient. When a specific nutrient is not available, bacteria may activate genes that code for proteins needed to build that nutrient out of other molecules. Prokaryotes may also activate or deactivate genes in response to heat, light, moisture, and other stimuli from the world around them. Turning genes on and off allows bacteria to respond to their environment and use their energy and nutrients efficiently.

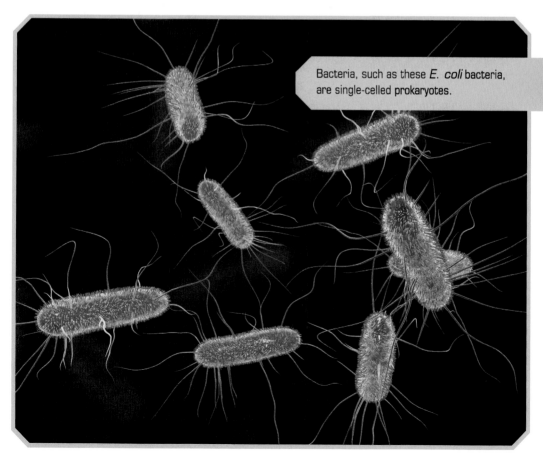

Bacteria, such as these *E. coli* bacteria, are single-celled prokaryotes.

Prokaryotes mainly regulate their genes using repressors, which reduce the amount of mRNA that is created from a gene. These proteins bind to the DNA near the beginning of the gene. They often make it so that RNA polymerase can't bind to the promoter, so that the gene is not transcribed.

E. coli is a type of bacteria found in the human intestines and is a favorite experimental subject for scientists. *E. coli* digests sugars, just like humans do. Under normal conditions, however, *E. coli* can't digest lactose, a sugar found in dairy products. One of the proteins involved in lactose digestion, called beta-galactosidase, breaks the lactose into two simpler sugars. When no lactose is present, *E. coli* regulates the beta-galactosidase gene so that the protein isn't produced.

E. coli has a repressor that blocks the transcription of the beta-galactosidase gene. When no lactose is present, this repressor binds to the DNA sequence near the beginning of the beta-galactosidase gene. When lactose is present and there's little of the normal food sugar glucose, the lactose itself binds to the repressor. The repressor can't bind to DNA when it has lactose bound to it, and this in turn allows transcription of the beta-galactosidase gene to occur.

E. coli, shown here growing in a petri dish, live in the human interstines. Some kinds of *E. coli* can cause stomach cramps, bloody diarrhea, and vomiting.

EUKARYOTIC CELL REGULATION

Eukaryotes regulate their genes in many different ways. The regulation can occur at many different points during transcription and translation. Unlike prokaryotes, which use repressors to turn genes off, eukaryotes use activators to turn genes on. These activators, known as transcription factors, are proteins. Not all cells contain all transcription factors. A muscle cell will contain a particular set, while a skin cell will contain a different set. This presence or absence of specific transcription factors creates differences in cells.

Some transcription factors are present in all cells but aren't active all the time. For example, almost all organisms have a set of genes that activate when the organism gets very hot. These are known as heat shock genes. The heat shock transcription factor controls them and is always present but it's only active when the temperature rises above a certain level.

Signals from molecules outside the cell can also activate transcription factors and genes. Two of these molecules include growth factors and hormones. The flood of hormones that comes during puberty causes many different changes. Teens grow taller and grow more body hair. Those who are biologically girls develop breasts and begin to menstruate. Those who are biologically boys voices deepen. All these changes occur because the hormones are activating transcription factors.

To have an effect, hormones must bind to specific receptors on or in the cell. Some hormones can't cross the cell membrane. Instead, they bind to receptors located on the cell's surface. This initiates a set of chemical reactions that causes the activation of a transcription factor. Other hormones can enter the cell and bind to transcription factors directly. Transcription factors are inactive until a hormone binds to them. With a hormone bound, however, they're active and will cause transcription to occur. Other hormones turn off, or inactivate, transcription factors by binding to them.

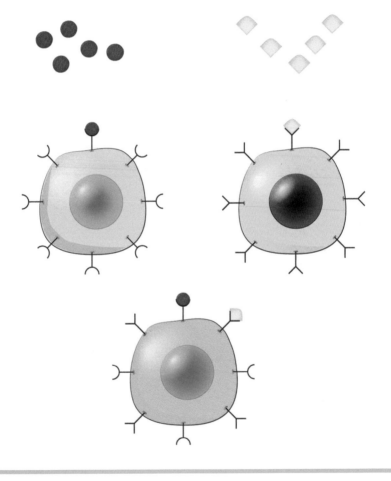

This diagram demostrates how certain cells have receptors for certain hormones (red and yellow).

Cells have many different ways of determining how much of which proteins are made. These methods focus on preventing the transcription or translation of the DNA or RNA. But what happens when something is wrong with the DNA? There are times when mutations can occur.

OTHER WAYS TO REGULATE EUKARYOTIC GENES

Preventing transcription seems like the most efficient way to regulate genes. Eukaryotes can also regulate genes farther down the path toward a protein. After an mRNA has been transcribed, it must be processed before it can be translated. One way that eukaryotes regulate genes is by not processing mRNAs. Eukaryotic cells can also regulate genes by not translating mRNAs. No protein can be made without translation. This kind of regulation often occurs during development. The egg cells of many animals, for example, contain a lot of mRNA, but these mRNAs aren't translated until after the egg is fertilized. Scientists are still figuring out how cells prevent translation from occurring until they're ready.

Many of the mRNAs, grouped in different parts of egg cells, code for transcription factors. When the egg is fertilized and starts dividing, these mRNAs end up in different cells. A cell will become muscle or skin or another type of cell depending on the transcription factors it contains. For this reason, RNA and transcription factors are extremely important for proper development of an organism because they appear to determine which genes are turned on and off in many cases.

RNA degradation is another way eukaryotic cells regulate their genes. All mRNA molecules are degraded after a few minutes to an hour. How quickly an mRNA is degraded depends on the sequence of the 3' untranslated region, or UTR. All mRNA molecules have this region on their 3' end that does not code for protein. The sequence AUUUA in the 3' UTR signals that the mRNA should be degraded quickly. Sometimes this sequence appears many times in the 3' UTR, which signals very fast degradation. Other mRNA molecules don't contain this sequence at all and they are degraded much more slowly.

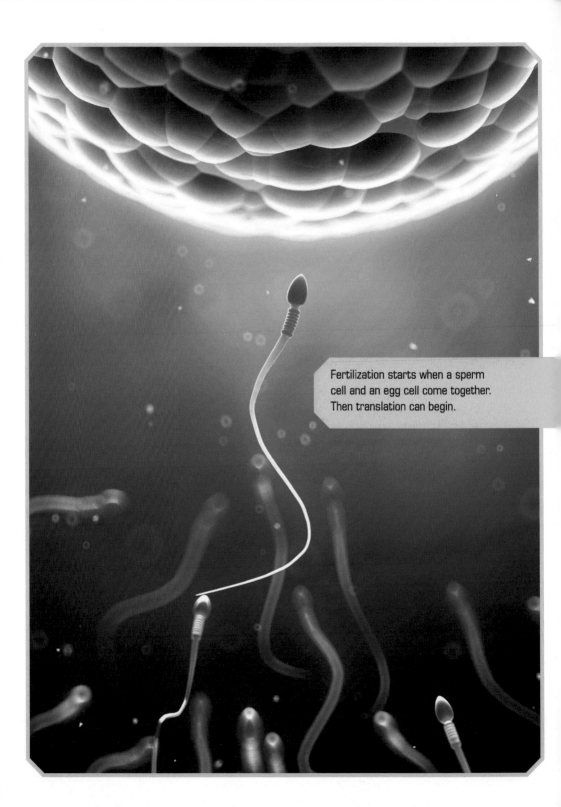

Fertilization starts when a sperm cell and an egg cell come together. Then translation can begin.

WHAT ARE MUTATIONS?

The word "mutation" often makes people think of horribly deformed creatures, such as three-eyed fish. Or you might be familiar with the term from comic books and superhero movies where characters get their superpowers through mutations. Most real-life mutations, however, are not nearly so dramatic.

A mutation is a change in the DNA sequence of an organism. The DNA replication process is precise but not perfect. Mistakes sometimes happen. These mistakes are mutations. Mutations can also result from exposure to radiation, certain chemicals, or particular viruses. People have ways of protecting themselves from mutations. Sunbathers wear sunscreen and sunglasses. Patients wear a lead vest during dental x-rays.

Lead is a very dense material. Therefore, it's able to block the radiation created by x-ray machines.

Some mutations are beneficial to an organism. A mutation inherited from a parent sometimes results in positive results. For example, an inherited mutation could cause a bird to have a narrower beak than others. This beak could allow the bird to reach nectar and seeds that other birds cannot reach. This could result in the bird getting more food to eat during times when food is scarce. The bird with the narrow beak may have a greater chance of surviving and having more babies than other birds. Some of the baby birds would also have the beneficial mutation, find hidden food sources, and have lots of babies. Over time, the bird population could come to mostly or entirely be made of individuals that had the mutation for a narrow beak. This is natural selection at work. Organisms that contain beneficial characteristics are more likely to reproduce, so over time these characteristics can become standard in the population.

Hummingbirds have evolved to have long, slender beaks. They use their beaks to reach the nectar inside flowers.

Other mutations have no effect at all on an organism. Without looking at the DNA code, no one will know that they are there. Still other mutations can cause disease and even death. Fortunately, new technologies are allowing us to test for these mutations and treat some diseases earlier.

SEQUENCE MUTATIONS

Several kinds of mutations can occur in a DNA sequence. The first, a point mutation, is a substitution of one base for another; for example, an A instead of a T. A point mutation can have three consequences. First, it may do nothing at all. The bases in DNA are transcribed into mRNA. And, in most cases, multiple codons in the mRNA correspond to the same amino acid. For example, UGC and UGU both code for cysteine. Therefore, a mutation that changes a UGU codon to UGC won't have any effect because the same amino acid ends up in the protein. This is known as a silent mutation.

However, changing a UGU codon to UGG means that tryptophan will be added to the protein instead of cysteine. This substitution of one amino acid for another is known as a missense mutation. The effect of a missense mutation depends on where the amino acid is located in the protein and what its role is.

Finally, changing a UGU codon to UGA leads to big problem. UGA is one of the three stop codons. This mutation will terminate transcription of the mRNA early. This is known as a nonsense mutation. Nonsense mutations almost always result in nonfunctional proteins.

Substitution of one base for another isn't the only way mutations can occur. Sometimes a base pair is added or deleted. This is easier to understand using words instead of codons. Think about the sentence: LET MAX THE DOG RUN. Say that the M is deleted. Starting with the same three-letter words, the sentence would then read LET AXT HED OGR UN, which is nonsense. The reading frame has been changed. An addition or subtraction of two base pairs also changes the reading frame. But addition or subtraction of three base pairs simply adds or deletes an amino acid. In the sentence above, say that M, A, and X were deleted. LET THE DOG RUN is shorter than the original, but it still makes sense. Sometimes adding or removing an amino acid will cause a big change in a protein. Other times it may have no effect.

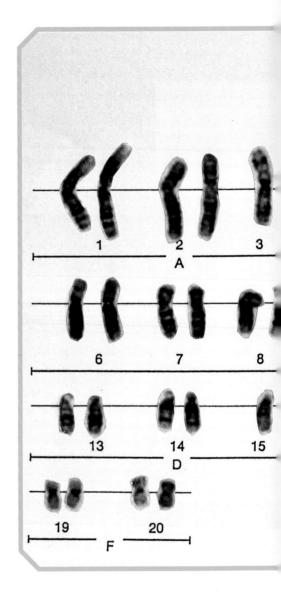

MUTATIONS TO CHROMOSOMES

Mutations can also occur when chromosomes swap DNA during meiosis. During meiosis, pieces of DNA that are the same size are supposed to be exchanged. Sometimes, however, chromosomes **exchange** strands of different sizes. This means that one chromosome is now missing genes, while the other chromosome has two copies. Other times, chromosomes will swap DNA of the same size, but the DNA attaches to the chromosome upside down. Or, sometimes the chromosomes don't separate properly during meiosis, and one sex cell ends up with two copies of a particular chromosome while another contains zero.

This is a karyotype, or a photograph of the chromosomes in a person's cells. This karyotype is from a male who has Down syndrome.

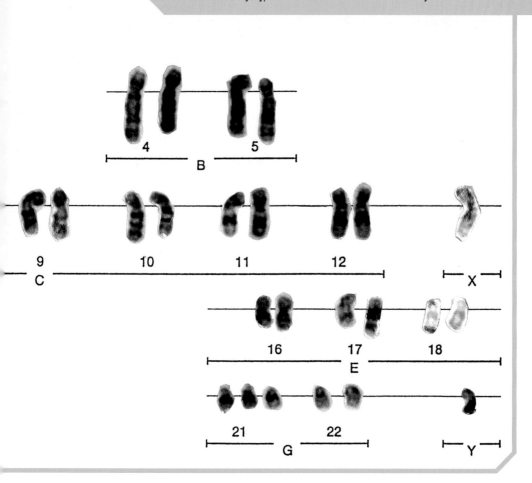

Chromosomal mutations can cause abnormalities in organisms. In fact, mothers pregnant with fetuses with these kinds of mutations often miscarry because the fetus is unable to survive. However, some chromosomal mutations don't result in death. For example, Down syndrome occurs when someone has three copies of chromosome 21.

CANCER–CAUSING MUTATIONS

Cancer can result when mutations occur in nonsex cells. This is particularly true for mutations in genes that code for growth factors, which are proteins that control the speed of cell division. Mutations in growth factors can cause cells to grow out of control, which is a characteristic of cancer. These mutations are often caused by exposure to radiation or chemicals.

Some mutated genes that make a person more likely to get cancer are hereditary. The mutations in the BRCA1 and BRCA2 genes are linked to breast cancer. Having mutations in these genes doesn't mean that someone will definitely get cancer, but it makes it more likely.

People can choose to be tested for mutations in the BRCA1 and BRCA2 genes, as well as others known to be asso-

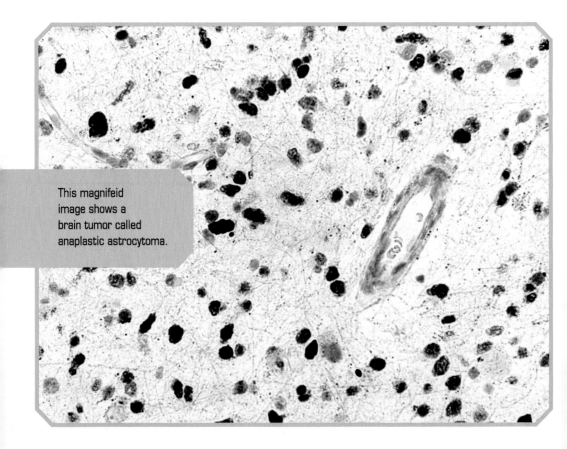

This magnifeid image shows a brain tumor called anaplastic astrocytoma.

TRACING HISTORY

Some scientists have used DNA mutations to trace the evolution and migration of humans in history. In eukaryotes, the nucleus isn't the only structure in the cell that contains DNA. The cells' mitochondria also have DNA. Mitochondria are passed from mothers to their children. If no mutations occur, a mother and her children will have exactly the same mitochondrial DNA.

In a 1987 article in the journal *Nature*, scientists looked at the mitochondrial DNA of people from different ethnic groups living in different parts of the world. They compared the sequences to discover which mutations were shared by many groups and which ones by few groups. Mutations shared by many groups must have occurred earlier than mutations shared by just a few groups because they had more generations to spread. They used this information to draw a "human family tree." This tree suggested that all living humans had a common ancestor that lived 140,000 to 290,000 years ago. Many people were shocked by this result. Scientists had believed that humans' common ancestor lived about 2 million years ago.

In 2000, another group of scientists did a similar study using DNA from Y-chromosomes. Only men have Y-chromosomes. If no mutations occur, a father and son will have exactly the same Y-chromosome. The human family tree found in this study was similar to the mitochondrial tree. It suggested a common ancestor about 150,000 years ago. This research has made scientists reconsider other evidence about early humans.

ciated with cancer or other diseases. People usually choose to be tested if they have a family history of a disease. If people do have a mutation, they may be able to take various steps to reduce their risk of developing the disease. They may also decide to use reproductive technologies to avoid passing the mutated gene down to their children.

GENETIC TESTING

Tests now exist for hundreds of diseases that have a genetic component. Many of these are used on unborn and newborn babies. The most common test for unborn babies is called amniocentesis. During this process, a physician extracts amniotic fluid from the uterus. This fluid, which cushions the fetus, contains fetal cells. Doctors analyze the DNA in these cells for mutations. If the test reveals that a baby has a severe genetic disorder, some parents may choose to not continue the pregnancy.

Babies have blood drawn to check for a wide variety of genetic diseases soon after birth. Most of these diseases are treatable with a special diet or medication. For example, phenyl-ketonuria (PKU) is a disease caused by a mutation in the gene for phenylalanine hydroxylase. This enzyme converts the amino acid phenylalanine into tyrosine, another amino acid. The mutated form of the enzyme is not functional. The buildup of phenylalanine in the bodies of people with PKU causes intellectual disabilities. However, if people with this disorder follow a diet low in phenylalanine, much of the damage can be avoided.

Today, people all over the world can order a DNA test kit from a number of companies. Most require you to swab the inside of your cheek and send the sample to a lab for genetic testing.

CHAPTER 6

WHAT IS RECOMBINANT DNA?

Researchers have developed many different techniques related to DNA. One of the most powerful creates recombinant DNA. It is created by inserting one or more genes from one organism into another organism. This allows the organism with the new gene to make proteins that it normally wouldn't make. Or, the recombinant DNA technique can be used to replace a nonfunctional copy of a gene with a functional one from the same type of organism. Recombinant DNA has a wide variety of uses in agriculture, medicine, and scientific research. Despite its usefulness, recombinant DNA technology is also a hotly debated topic.

This simple diagram demonstrates how the DNA from one organism can be introduced to another organism to create recombinant DNA.

THE RECIPE FOR RECOMBINANT DNA

The process of creating an organism containing recombinant DNA has many steps. Let's say, for example, that a scientist wants to insert a human gene into a bacterium. First, proteins called restriction endonucleases separate the human gene from its normal location on a chromosome. Restriction endonucleases cut DNA only at specific sequences. The scientist needs to know the sequence of the gene and the DNA around it. Then the scientist can choose restriction endonucleases that will cut the DNA before and after the gene, but not in the middle.

Scientists have worked for years researching DNA and experimenting with recombinant gene technology.

At this point, many copies of the gene are created. This is done with a technique called the polymerase chain reaction, or PCR. Using this process, the DNA is first heated nearly to boiling, which splits the double helix into two single-stranded pieces. Primers are added as the mixture cools. Primers are short strands of nucleotides that are complementary to short stretches of the gene. The primers bind to the DNA. When the mixture reaches 131 degrees Fahrenheit (55 degrees Celsius), DNA polymerase is added. Most DNA polymerases don't work at this high temperature, but the DNA polymerase used is taken from a bacterium that lives in hot springs. This DNA polymerase attaches nucleotides to the DNA so that it becomes double-stranded again. Then the entire cycle begins again. Using PCR, scientists can make millions of copies of a DNA sequence in just a few hours.

Next, the gene is inserted into the bacterium's DNA. Scientists remove DNA from bacterial cells. The same restriction endonucleases used to snip out the human gene are used to open up a hole in the bacterium's DNA. The enzyme DNA ligase is used to connect the human gene with the bacterial DNA. Then scientists need to insert the recombinant DNA back into a living bacterium. Scientists perform various techniques to make bacteria more likely to take up DNA from the environment. Researchers have used other methods to insert DNA into other types of cells. Some have employed "gene guns" that actually force DNA through cell membranes. Others have loaded the DNA into viruses, which then infect cells. These viruses are altered so they deliver the DNA without destroying the cell. Once the DNA is in the cell, it should begin making the protein that the gene codes for.

PROTEIN FACTORIES

Recombinant DNA has many uses. You've already read that it can be used to make large amounts of proteins. These proteins are usually medically or industrially important. For example, recombinant DNA technology is used to make insulin. Insulin is a protein produced by the pancreas that's important for regulating blood sugar. People with some forms of diabetes have trouble regulating the level of insulin in their bodies, so they must regularly inject insulin into their bodies. This insulin used to come from pigs and cows. Insulin from these animals is very similar to human insulin, but some people had allergic reactions to it. After recombinant DNA was invented, researchers inserted the gene for human insulin into a bacterium. This was not an easy process. Human genes contain introns that are later snipped out. Bacterial genes don't have introns. Because of this, bacteria don't have the spliceosomes needed to edit out introns. Therefore, researchers had to create a copy of the insulin gene that was free of introns to insert into the bacteria.

After they've taken up the recombinant DNA, the bacteria then undergo cell division, creating many tiny factories for producing insulin. The insulin is collected, purified, and shipped to patients. Several other proteins, including human growth hormone, have also been made in large quantities using recombinant DNA.

GENETICALLY MODIFIED ORGANISMS

For thousands of years, farmers have been breeding plants and animals to obtain desirable traits. However, recombinant DNA technology allows researchers to insert genes that provide these characteristics.

Organisms that contain recombinant DNA are often called genetically modified organisms (GMOs). These organisms are particularly of use—and concern—in agriculture. Golden rice is an example of a GMO. In underdeveloped countries, many children lack vitamin A in their diet, which can cause blindness. Rice is a staple crop in some underdeveloped countries. Rice plants make beta-carotene, a precursor to vitamin A, in their leaves—but not in the grain. Researchers inserted two genes into a rice cell. These two genes allow the rice plant to make beta-carotene in the grain. The rice is a golden color instead of white because of the beta-carotene. The human body converts the beta-carotene to vitamin A. The scientists believe that golden rice could help prevent thousands of children from going blind.

A variety of other GMOs exist. Many of these GMOs have extra genes that provide resistance to pests or herbicides. Roundup Ready crops, for example, are resistant to the herbicide Roundup. Farmers growing Roundup Ready crops can use Roundup to kill weeds in their fields without worrying that they will kill their crops as well.

GMO DEBATE: REVOLUTIONARY DISCOVERY OR FRANKENFOOD?

The process of recombinant DNA is used to create genetically modified foods. You might be surprised to hear that some of your favorite crops grown in the United States are largely genetically modified organisms, or GMOs. For example, in 2018, approximately 94 percent of the soybeans, 94 percent of the cotton, and 92 percent of the corn grown in the United States were genetically modified crops. GMO crops are often designed to resist pests tolerate chemical pesticides.

Do you want to eat foods that contain foreign DNA? Many people have decided that they don't. Genetically modified organisms have been called "frankenfood" by some people. People worry that these organisms' long-term safety has not been studied enough. They also fear that growing GMO crops will result in negative effects for the environment. Others say that GMO foods are completely safe. In fact, some of these crops are more nutritious or require fewer pesticides. Whether or not to eat GMOs is a decision that each person should make for themselves after reviewing the available evidence.

The United States is the world's leading grower of soybeans. Soybeans are the world's largest source of animal feed and the second-largest source of vegetable oil.

GENE THERAPY

Gene therapy is a developing technology that aims to change the outcome of certain diseases through recombinant DNA. The process includes introducing a functional gene into the human body to take the place of a mutated or nonfunctional gene. Gene therapy is difficult because a lot of cells must take up the gene. Bacteria are single-celled organisms, so the new gene only needs to get into one cell. When creating genetically modified crops, the new gene can be put into sperm or egg cells. Then it ends up in all of the cells of the new organism. Putting a gene into a complex organism, like a grown human who is already alive and contains millions of cells that need the gene, is a different story altogether.

Since many proteins are only important in certain types of cells, the gene may not need to be inserted in every type of cell. But even if gene therapy is limited to one type of cell, that's still a lot of cells.

Most gene therapy uses RNA-based viruses to get genes into cells. Once in a cell, the RNA is reverse transcribed to DNA, which is inserted into a chromosome. The RNA-based viruses used in gene therapy are engineered so they only contain the RNA for the new gene and the components necessary to enter the cell and insert the new DNA into the cell's genome. They're not supposed to be able to cause infection.

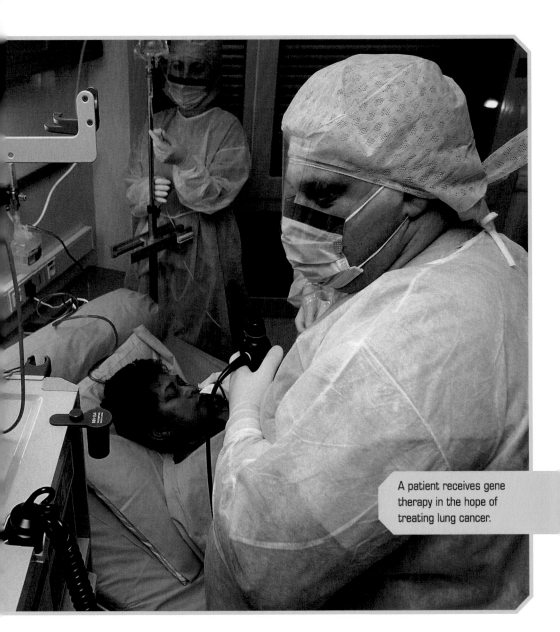

A patient receives gene therapy in the hope of treating lung cancer.

Early trials in gene therapy were not very successful. Patients died or became very sick in some of these trials, so they ended early. However, many researchers are working hard to develop successful gene therapies. It's interesting to note that the FDA has already approved some gene therapy drugs, mostly for the treatment of specific cancers.

GLOSSARY

AMINO ACID The building block of proteins.

ARCHAEA Usually single-celled prokaryotes that live near hot springs and deep sea vents. The singular is archaeon.

BASE One of the building blocks of DNA and RNA; can be adenine, thymine, cytosine, guanine, or uracil.

CATALYST A substance used to speed up a reaction.

CHROMOSOME A long segment of DNA specific to a particular type of organism.

CODON A set of three bases in RNA that specify a particular amino acid.

DNA Deoxyribonucleic acid, the molecule that contains genetic information.

DOUBLE HELIX The two-stranded, twisted shape of a DNA molecule.

ENZYME A molecule, usually a protein but sometimes RNA, that helps two other molecules react with each other.

GENE A stretch of DNA that contains the instructions to make a protein.

GENOME An organism's full complement of genes.

HISTONES The proteins that protect DNA and help it fold up in the nucleus.

MEIOSIS The process of dividing a cell into four sex cells, each with half an organism's usual amount of DNA.

MITOSIS The process of dividing a cell into two new cells, each with an organism's usual amount of DNA.

MUTATION A rare change in a DNA sequence.

NUCLEIC ACID DNA and RNA.

NUCLEUS The location of DNA in eukaryotic cells.

PHOSPHATE A component of the backbone of DNA that contains phosphorus and oxygen.

POLYMERASE CHAIN REACTION (PCR) A method of obtaining millions of copies of a DNA sequence in a short period of time.

PROTEIN Molecules made of amino acids that do the work of a cell.

RECOMBINANT DNA DNA that is created by combining DNA from two organisms.

REPLICATION The process of creating a copy of all DNA in a cell in preparation for cell division.

RIBOSOME A structure made of protein and RNA where proteins are made in the cell.

RNA Ribonucleic acid, a molecule that is central to the synthesis of proteins.

TRANSCRIPTION The process of creating an RNA molecule from a DNA molecule.

TRANSLATION The process of creating a protein based on the information in an RNA molecule.

FOR MORE INFORMATION

AMERICAN SOCIETY FOR BIOCHEMISTRY AND MOLECULAR BIOLOGY (ASBMB)
11200 Rockville Pike, Suite 302
Rockville, MD 20852-3110
(240) 283-6600
Website: www.asbmb.org
This organization publishes scientific journals, advocates for funding for research, and supports science education, all with an emphasis on biochemistry and molecular biology.

AMERICAN SOCIETY OF GENE CELL THERAPY (ASGCT)
20800 Swenson Dr.
Suite 300
Waukesha, WI 53186
(414) 278-1341
Website: www.asgt.org
This medical and scientific organization helps scientists and the public understand genetic and cellular therapies.

AMERICAN SOCIETY OF HUMAN GENETICS (ASHG)
6120 Executive Boulevard Suite 500
Rockville, MD 20852
(301) 634-7300
Website: www.ashg.org
This organization hosts conferences, advocates for support for genetic research, promotes genetic services, and educates the public about genetics.

CANADIAN ASSOCIATION OF GENETIC COUNSELLORS (CAGC)
P.O. Box 52083
Oakville, ON L6J 7N5
Canada

(905) 847-1363
Website: www.cagc-accg.ca
This organization educates the public about genetic counseling and supports genetic counselors. Genetic counselors help people who are undergoing genetic testing understand their options.

GENETICS SOCIETY OF AMERICA (GSA)

6120 Executive Boulevard
Suite 550
Rockville, MD 20852
(240) 880-2000
Website: www.genetics-gsa.org
This organization brings together geneticists, promotes research in genetics, helps train new geneticists, and educates the public and government about advances in genetics and their potential consequences.

NATIONAL HUMAN GENOME RESEARCH INSTITUTE (NHGRI)

National Institutes of Health (NIH)
Building 31, Room 4B09
31 Center Drive, MSC 2152
9000 Rockville Pike
Bethesda, MD 20892-2152
(301) 402-0911
Website: www.genome.gov
NHGRI collaborates with the scientific and medical communities to facilitate genomic breakthroughs and supports the study and treatment of specific diseases. This organization is focused on contributing to high-impact research and helping to apply new discoveries to the study of human health.

NATIONAL SOCIETY OF GENETIC COUNSELORS (NSGC)

330 North Wabash Avenue
Suite 2000
Chicago, IL 60611
(312) 321-6834
Website: www.nsgc.org
This organization supports education, research, and public policy regarding genetic counseling in the United States.

FOR FURTHER READING

Allman, Toney. *Changing Lives Through Genetic Engineering*. San Diego, CA: Referencepoint Press, 2020.

Arney, Kat. *Exploring the Human Genome*. New York, NY: Rosen Publlishing, 2019.

Bae, Yea Jee. *Pesticides and GMOs*. New York, NY: Greenhaven Publishing, 2019.

Denton, Michelle. *Genetic Engineering and Genetically Modified Organisms*. New York, NY: Lucent Press, 2019.

Folkersen, Lasse. *Understand Your DNA: A Guide*. Hackensack, NJ: World Scientific, 2019.

Irving, Melita, Dr. *The Human DNA Manual: Understanding Your Genetic Code*. Newbury Park, CA: Haynes Publishing, 2019.

Lewis, Ricki. *Human Genetics: The Basics*. New York, NY: Routledge, 2017.

Lew, Kristi. *Genetic Ancestry Testing*. New York, NY: Enslow Publishing, 2018.

Lew, Kristi. *Taxonomy: The Classification of Biological Organisms*. New York, NY: Enslow Publishing, 2018.

Lew, Kristi. *Understanding the Human Genome*. New York, NY: Enslow Publishing, 2018.

Mooney, Carla. *The Human Genome: Mapping the Blueprint of Human Life*. White River Junction, VT: Nomad Press, 2020.

Rauf, Don. *DNA, RNA, and the Inheritance of Traits*. New York, NY: Enslow Publishing, 2018.

Ridge, Yolanda. *CRISPR: A Powerful Way to Change DNA*. Toronto, ON, Canada: Annick Press, 2020.

Roberts, Alice, et al. *Evolution: The Human Story*. New York, NY: DK Publishing, 2018.

Robinson, Tara Rodden. *Genetics for Dummies (third edition)*. Hoboken, NJ: John Wiley & Sons, 2020.

Stuart, Whitney, and Hans C. Andersson, MD. *Genomics: A Revolution in Health and Disease Discovery*. Minneapolis, MN: Twenty-First Century Books, 2021.

Wilmer, George. Gregor Mendel. Broomall, PA: Mason Crest Publishers, 2018.

INDEX

PHOTO CREDITS